Transform Your Business with Strategic Online Marketing

7 Proven Online Solutions for Driving New Clients to YOUR Local Business

By: Burke Walker & Jeff Lerner

www.Xurli.com

www.Xurli.com

ISBN-13: 9781517044282

This publication is designed to provide general information
regarding the subject matter covered. However, laws and
practices often vary from state to state and country to country are
subject to change. Because each factual situation is different,
specific advice should be tailored to the particular circumstances.
For this reason, the reader is advised to consult with an advisor
regarding that individual's specific situation.

The author has taken reasonable precautions in the preparation of
this book and believes that the facts as presented in this work are
accurate as of the date written. However, neither the author nor
the publisher assumes any responsibility for any errors or
omissions. The author specifically disclaims any liability
resulting from the use or application of the information contained

in this book, and the information is not intended to serve as legal advice related to individual situations.

Xurli focuses first on online presence optimization and then strategic online marketing solutions for their clients to set them apart in their area… and transform their status to elevate them as an industry expert and obvious choice for service.

If you are ready to take your business or practice to the next level, visit our site at **www.Xurli.com** and register for an in depth marketing analysis for your business.

XURLI.com/marketinganalysis

Table of Contents

Why It's Now Harder To Get New Customers

Local businesses are seeing more competition for customers, clients, and patients than ever before. A recent Small Business Administration study reports that local businesses are seeing the largest increase in years.

Since 1990, large corporations have eliminated 4 million jobs and local businesses have added 8 million new jobs.
The number of local businesses has increased 49% since 1982... that is nearly 12 million new businesses that are all competing for customers.

But it Gets Worse!

Recent statistics show that even after coming out of the hard economic times of the past several years, many local businesses are struggling to survive and many will go out of business in the next 3-5 years.

To make matters worse, recent statistics show that most local businesses are relying on traditional methods of getting clients and those methods have stopped working...

Good News: There Are Still Plenty of Customers Out There!

It's true and I can tell you that if you are ready to take your business to the next level, the information I am about to share could be worth a fortune to you!

The good news is that it is very likely that you will be able to implement these strategies without having to spend any more than you already are on advertising. (Don't worry if you aren't spending any money on advertising I will show you very low-cost effective ways to get your message in front of people hungry for your product or service)

New Customer Getting Methods

So how do you get more customers? Of course there is traditional advertising, cold calling, networking etc. But these are the things that most businesses have been doing from the start and so has the competition.

We need to breathe some fresh air into this area of your business. There are actually 34 methods that can be leveraged to get more clients, but that would probably overwhelm most business owners and I want to give you a few of the most effective ways so you can start and get some success under your belt.

Here is the initial list I work from for my consulting clients:

- Online Presence Management
- Search Engine Optimization
- SMARTsites
- Google AdWords
- Google+ and Online Directories
- Mobile Marketing
- Mobile Apps

- YouTube Marketing
- Social Media Marketing - Facebook
- LinkedIn
- Blogging
- Content / Educational Marketing
- Direct Response Marketing
- Power of Referral Strategies
- Reputation Management
- Branding and Logo Strategies
- Trade Publications
- Trade Show Marketing
- Direct Mail

Whew... Big Sigh... That's a lot of stuff to jump on right out of the gate... I thought you said just a few. Well the fact is that *is* we will only look closely at less than half of the methods.

Let's look at a few that you can implement and get some quick momentum, no matter what type of business you have... because I am passionate about simplifying the Internet for Local Business owners.

It doesn't matter if you are selling a physical product, a service or an information product, the methods I am about to share will work for you to make your business or practice more appealing...and attract more clients.

Quick Note on Cleaning Up Past Mistakes:

What kind of mistakes?

There are a few things businesses often have hanging over them from past marketing efforts that can penalize them according to current standards online. The search engines are very specific about what they like and don't like when it comes to directory listings and websites. Failure to comply with the current standards can have a dramatic negative impact on how often a business is shown in local search. I'll address those pitfalls as well.

Spreading the Word: Promoting Your Business!

If you look at traditional advertising like Yellow Pages, the newspaper or TV commercials these platforms all have one thing in common. They are expensive and there is no real way to measure their effectiveness.

Let's look first at the Yellow Pages... let me ask you a question...

Do you know where your yellow pages book is right now? My guess is that you don't, as a matter of fact you may not even have one in your office. When was the last time you looked in the yellow pages for a business? If you are like me, it was a few years ago.

Even though this is commonplace, many businesses still spend thousands each year on yellow page ads. Studies show that the average of a person who uses yellow pages is over 70 years of age... So if this is not your target market...

then you marketing dollars may be more effective with newer methods.

I look at TV commercials and Newspaper ads as a place where you spend money telling people all about your product or service and hope they either need it at the exact moment they see the advertisement or remember your ad when they do need your service.

Here is a question about the newspaper...Do you get the local paper on a daily basis?

Again, my guess is probably not, and it is a safe guess because 24 of the top 25 newspapers have seen record declines in sales. I would also venture to guess that if you do place ads in the newspaper you can't tell me where I should look to find information about your business... that's because even though ads pay for the lion's share of the newspaper's publishing costs... they get placed where ever there is space left after the articles are all laid out for maximum readership.

When it comes to TV Commercials not only is it almost impossible to measure effectiveness, most people watch recorded shows these days and skip the commercials all together. So what is a business owner to do?

Start of a New Era: How the Internet Became Local

Businesses of all types and scopes are just really starting to become aware of what a small percentage of early adopters already know: Internet and mobile device platforms have revolutionized local business marketing.

Thanks to high-speed wireless networks, mobile devices, communications software, and social platforms, marketing has been transformed into a largely digital discipline for local businesses.

This new media is quickly replacing old school advertising methods such as newspaper ads, printed business directories like the Yellow Pages, direct mail coupons—even radio and TV ads.

Online marketing is also effective whether or not a business currently sells products or services over the Internet. "Brick and mortar" businesses of all kinds are using these new strategies with impressive results.

Local consumers increased usage of the Internet and mobile media is driving businesses to learn how to take advantage of these new platforms so their prospects and customers can find them, hear about them and, ultimately, buy from them.

This is also important because the Internet is now interactive. Consumers are sharing their experiences with local businesses... Both positive and negative! Not only is it very important for business owners to know to control the message that they're putting out, but they must also keep track of what people are saying about their business.

Take a look at the statistics: Google has over 3.5 billion searches every day; out of those 3.5 billion searches over 28 billion a month (or in 27% of all searches) are local. What that means is people are actually putting in a geographic identifier in the search bar.

For instance if you're in St George and you're looking for a dentist, chances are you don't just put in "dentist"; chances are you put in "St George dentist" or "St George dental office." You type something that identifies where you are geographically.

From there the search engine knows to go find the information that's most relevant for you. After all, if you have a toothache, you don't really care about how great the dentist in Atlanta is if you live in Orlando. The same thing goes for a pizza joint. If you're looking for pizza, you probably aren't looking for just pizza in general; you're looking for it based on where you're located.

Here's another amazing statistic: 82% of local searches are followed by an action, a store visit, a call, an email or a purchase. So when people are searching locally, it means they're ready to take an action and more likely to buy. They are a purchase driven consumer!

XURLI.com/marketinganalysis

Gaining Local Market Share: Capitalizing on Local Searches

The great news is there are a number of ways that we can put information online for people to find when they're searching locally. Local Internet marketing is based on helping local business owners put information online where people can find it at the exact time that they're looking for it. That's very important and it's very different than other forms of advertising.

For instance, look at the yellow pages. Stop and ask yourself this question: do you know where your phone book is right now? Probably not... If you're like 80% of the population, you don't have a clue where that giant book is. The average age of someone who uses yellow pages is over 70 years of age. This means if a business is in the yellow pages alone, they are missing out on the vast majority of the population.

Remember the Internet uses a technological way of finding the most relevant information about businesses, and nearly everyone uses it. Old school methods just don't produce enough results to even pay for themselves anymore.

Alternatively local Internet marketing provides a strategy for local businesses to put their information in hundreds of places so that people can find the information at exact time that they need the product or service.

Both in theory and in practice, this has proven to be a much better solution and makes it much easier for the business owner to see the value of their advertising funds rather than just continuing to spend thousands of dollars on ineffective means of marketing.

Preselling Your Business Online - Building a Great Website to Kick Start Your Internet Marketing Plan

Preselling your business online is important; in order to make it work, you'll need a great website... or even better, a SMARTsite. In fact, a robust site can actually be the key to the beginning of your internet marketing campaign. When you begin looking at the task of promotion, it helps to understand what all is involved in the process. You want to generate highly targeted, qualified customers. To do this, you'll need a great-looking, functional website that will garner traffic.

There are several aspects that make up a successful Internet marketing plan. They should be the building blocks of your campaign. You need to generate interest. Knowing what your target audience wants is the key to giving them content that will be of interest to them. Since you are marketing via the Internet, you'll be selling the idea of your business to visitors who are seeking the type of information you have to offer. This can serve you well because it takes the guesswork out of figuring out what they need to know. You'll need to include this information on your website. It should be informative and easy to read.

Educate your visitors. Give them something they can use. Instead of just recycling the same information found on other similar websites, make yours unique. Tell your visitors something that will be relevant and important. This is what will keep them coming back time after time.

Create desire. A strategically developed SMARTsite should give them the desire to want to know more. Keep the content interesting and fresh. Include any new information relevant to the topics pertaining to services offered by your business or practice.

When you presell your business online, you are preparing your prospects for what is offered on your website. Email marketing is also a great way to get prospects to your site. While the SMARTsite itself is the starting point for your internet marketing plan, the emails you send will be used to entice people into becoming visitors.

Know your market. When you understand who you are talking to, knowing what to tell them will be easier. Your site should be based on your target market. Consider who will likely visit your site. Ask yourself what they will want to know.

Use examples or scenarios on your SMARTsite. This gives your readers something to relate to in a very direct way. If what you wrote describes that person, you have just come that much closer to gaining a customer. This allows you to create the needed interest that will draw your prospect closer. Include different scenarios. Not all your prospects will be in the same situation. In fact, some may be very different. You can appeal to a wider range of patients by including a number of scenarios.

Make sure the information on your site is clear. Your readers should have no problem understanding your information. Use language that makes sense to the masses. If you must use industry jargon, be sure to explain it. Only use industry language when necessary. Otherwise, explain things in terms that are easy to comprehend. You want your customers to relate to you on a very personal level. This is what will cause a peak in their interest and keep them coming back.

Here are some examples of the 'past mistakes' or shortcomings I referenced at the beginning:

- 1) Having a non-responsive (e.g., mobile and tablet friendly) website linked to the listing;
- 2) Using cheap "mobile site generators" to reshuffle the site's content into a separate mobile-version;
- 3) Letting the phone company generate the website and use tracking phone numbers to track leads;
- 4) Having improper formatting of key elements in the website;
- 5) Having inconsistencies between the website and the directory listing;
- 6) Having too many keywords on the listing;
- 7) Having too few keywords or poor keyword relevance on the listing; and
- 8) Having redundant listings or websites that many businesses don't even know are out there.
  These are just a few of the dozens of things that limit many businesses' potential online exposure.

Converting SMARTsite Visitors to Buyers

The key to a successful SMARTsite is conversion. You ultimately want those who visit your website to become customers/clients/patients. You will need a plan of action in order to make this happen. This plan will enable you to build relationships and create the trust necessary to increase the number of visitors you receive, but to also make them stay. Below are tips that will show you how to implement a site designed with conversion in mind.

Provide quality content about the products and services offered at your business. Make sure it is clear and concise. Information that is easy to understand will appeal to visitors, especially those who are conducting an initial search. Grab your visitor's attention immediately. This means putting the most important information first. Think of the main points you want them to be aware of and make sure these are incorporated before everything else.

Create a SMARTsite that is easy to navigate. Confusing layouts or content that is difficult to follow will prompt visitors to go elsewhere for information. Write all content with your potential patients in mind. Explain what you can do for them and how helpful your services will be. List the benefits of your services and tell them why they should choose your business.

Design your site specific for the target audience. This means creating each page with the respective types of visitors in mind. For example, you might link a specific page to a particular ad. That page might contain information about the services you offer. So, if a visitor is searching specifically for this type of information, it needs to be very easily accessible so clients can reach it both quickly and easily. This will take the guesswork out of navigating the entire site just to find the information they want.

On the other hand, another visitor might be reading an article about the benefits of your products and services and see a direct link to your home page. That person isn't necessarily looking for a specific type of information, but rather is searching for something more general. It's all about directing visitors to the right site, and you can use your various advertising mediums to target specific pages.

Implement active thinking... Use an active voice in all your content to keep your visitors motivated. Your copy should be engaging and make them want to continue reading. This is a more dynamic approach and often makes people feel as if they are being spoken to directly. It helps establish a rapport, which can quickly lead to a conversion.

Increase the trust between you and your visitors. Trust is the basis of any good relationship, and when it comes to promoting your business, it will serve you well. You want your prospects to believe in you and feel confident about the services you provide.

An effective website begins with a successful online marketing plan. Your business will greatly benefit from well-thought out pages designed specifically with your target market in mind. Use the tips above to build a website that will help your business grow.

The Top Five Benefits of Having a Great SMARTsite

A great SMARTsite is the most important online marketing tool you can have for your business. It's where much of the relevant information will be located and is your direct link to potential prospects. There are several benefits to having a well-developed site. Below are five of the most important advantages and why they are relevant:

Benefit #1

A great site is essential, it has become a requirement of sorts. Customers expect and look for it. They want to know there is a specific place they can go to get information.

If you fail to establish an Internet presence, your competition will beat you in the online marketing department. Your site can make you stand out from the rest and it should depict what your business is all about. Tell readers about the services you offer and how they can contact you. Your website should be informative and easy to read and navigate.

Benefit #2

A great SMARTsite helps build trust. It shows your visitors you have something important to offer and gives them a place to go where they can learn more. It is where you will have the chance to build your online image. It also shows your expertise in the field.

Benefit #3

A great SMARTsite increases the odds of others learning about your business. Now that many people are turning to the Internet for obtaining information, it is being relied upon to produce results. These results are produced by search engines.

The ultimate goal is to receive high rankings for all your pages. The more individual pages that rank high on your site, the more visible you'll be online. For this, search engine optimization (SEO) is key. The content of your site should incorporate keywords potential patients will use to find you. A well optimized site will place you high in the rankings.

Benefit #4

Design your site carefully. While you definitely want to keep the content easy to read and navigate, all your pages should be eye-catching. Many people choose a particular theme for their site. This helps give it a uniform look throughout.

Choose a theme or look that is relevant to what you are offering. Consider usability while making sure the content and all elements will grab the attention of visitors. A well-designed site that is easy to navigate and contains useful information will prompt them to stay.

Benefit #5

A great SMARTsite will give a great first impression. This is very important, especially to those who are hearing of you for the first time online. You need pages that look professional, are user-friendly, and will provide your potential customers with everything they'll need to begin taking advantage of your services.

Always include up-to-date information. This is absolutely essential. A site that hasn't been updated in a while will detract from your credibility in the eyes of visitors. You want it to look like there's been activity and you want that activity to be real. Add some useful articles or blog posts. This will show that you visit the site frequently and are in touch with the needs of your patients.

Make sure all contact information is correct. Visitors who are unable to make contact with questions will often go elsewhere. You can avoid this by providing several ways in which they may get in touch. Your website will serve you well if it receives the right attention. Think of it as a part of your overall business and allow it to grow with you.

XURLI.com/marketinganalysis

Why Great SMARTsite Copy Is Essential

Your site should contain great copy for several reasons. Presenting information the right way is what will get you high search engines rankings. These high rankings are what will enable people to find you. If you rank near (or at) the top, you will receive more hits than if you rank in the middle or the bottom. Many web users often don't make it very far down a results page before trying a new search. Most people don't like to search through hundreds of results and simply don't do it. That is why having a high website ranking is crucial. You want to be seen at the top.

The key is getting several pages to rank high. This allows you to take up several of the spots near the top. This will result in your name and URL being seen multiple times. Users will often click on a name they repeatedly see.

Great site copy presents a call to action. It clearly informs the user of what to do. For example, you might include a page on your site listing the benefits your services provide to your customers. This should be done in such a way that will prompt them to contact you to learn more. If the benefits are listed very clearly on your page, they should be easy to understand. The same is true for whatever action you want them to take.

Great site copy also evokes emotion. You want your visitors to feel something when they go to your site. Many may not be familiar with exactly what services you offer, and upon finding out, may feel a particular emotion. Perhaps it's hope or maybe even excitement because they finally have found the information they need. No matter what it is, you have made a difference. While it is about what you say, it's also about how you say it.

Your site copy should also tell compelling stories. These can come in the form of testimonials. People often respond well upon hearing about the experiences of others. You might even explain why you decided to open your business and tell readers about your expertise in the field.

When writing your copy, tell your stories in a way that will speak directly to your visitors. This is one of the easiest ways to turn a prospect into a customer. This is also a great way to gain trust. Prospects will want to come to you if they feel you know what you are doing and will take good care of them.

Your site copy is what will help establish your online credibility. You must write content that will inform, convince, identify with your visitor, and inspire a particular action to be taken. This often leads to the sharing of such information. A visitor who has become a customer may then recommend others to visit your website and, ultimately, your business. Your online presence should expand your business. It can help you reach people who aren't in close proximity to you, but who might greatly benefit from the services you have to offer.

Getting Traffic to Your Business: Tools Needed To Get Started With Local Online Marketing

There are 7 major strategies for creating a dominating local online presence. We will discuss each in great detail in the following chapters. When properly executed each of the strategies can bring new customers to your local business. When you combine these strategies you create a formidable presence for your business.

Strategy #1: Search Engine Optimization – Elevating and Ensuring Your Page Ranking

Search Engine Optimization (SEO) makes a website more desirable to the search engines. The main ways to optimize a website are through creating great content, specific keywords that are searched for on a regular basis, interaction on your website from people visiting and you also want to have other sites pointing to your website (which is called back linking).

When Google or one of the other search engine crawls (looks at) a website and it sees that there are other reputable websites (referred to as authority sites) that have links pointing to your website, they go, "Hey, other sites think this is important, so this site must be important," and it moves the site up the search rankings. The other important key is to have links out to other high-ranking authority sites like CNN, YouTube, etc. When the search engines see that your site is pointing to some of these other high ranking sites that have great information it helps to move your site up in the rankings.

The other part about SEO is using keywords. What are the words that you want to show up for when people are searching? When it comes to local marketing, it's not as hard as you may think. You can ask the first 10 people you run into, "if you were looking for a dentist in Atlanta, what words would you type in to the search engine?" More than likely if you ask 10 people, those are the top 10 things that people would probably search for.

With local marketing that's about as complicated as you need to get with keyword research. Now, there are a lot of tools out there that can go very in-depth but I would say you could very easily use the keyword tool that's available in any search engine to look at how many searches people are actually doing and how strong the competition is.

Previously the majority of website rankings were based on technical attributes. Things like On-page SEO, overuse of keywords (keyword stuffing), backlinks etc. previously helped your websites ranking. Now Content Creation is King. Google is now friendlier to original content than purchased traffic. The search engines use an ever-changing algorithm to determine what shows up on the first page. Today they reward originality of quality content and visitor interaction (time on site) more so than the number or backlinks.

KeyWord Research – What Are Your Prospects Looking For?

Keywords are the foundation of SEO. Keywords are the exact terms consumers are using to find what they are searching for. Single keywords are too broad of a search term for local searches. Three to Five words together are known as "long tail keyword phrases" are more powerful for local searches since they usually include a geographic identifier. These are usually used for very specific searches and have higher conversions.

Optimizing your website with long tail keywords is very important. By placing 4 to 6 long tail keywords in your website's code and in the page titles can help your websites ranking. An example of a single keyword would be the term "marketing". An example of a long tail keyword would be "Social Media Marketing Seattle, WA". As you can tell someone using the single keyword is looking for general information on marketing. The person using the long tail keyword phrase is going to find specific results for the social media marketing agencies in Seattle.

When creating content for Facebook, Twitter, blogs, YouTube, etc. always use your keywords in the title first. Content Creation with relevant keywords will help your website's organic ranking, and remember to avoid overstuffing. Overstuffing is excessive use of keywords and is frowned upon by search engines.

A great way to find out the best keywords to use for your website or content is by using Google's free keyword tool. You can research your specific keywords and it will make suggestions of keyword terms that are closely related to your search terms. The keyword planner will show you how many searches each term get per month. This can help you identify the best terms to use so that the most people will see your information. It will also show you which keywords are rated low, medium and highly competitive. This is important because it will be easier to rank for the low to medium competition keywords.

Strategy #2: Pay Per Click – Google AdWords…and Facebook

Advertising on Google is done by placing your ads in front of people who are actively searching for a term or "keyword" related to your product of service.

You are charged each time someone clicks on your ad. When they click on your ad it takes them to the web page you want them to see that will lead them to an engagement and making a purchase from you.

Let's look at an example of a company that sells Pool Supplies. They want their ads to show up in front of people who are actively searching for information about "pool supplies". We don't know exactly what type of information they are looking for, we just know they are they are searching the term "Albany Pool Supplies".

The ads show up at the Top of the Results page and along the right hand side of the page similar to Facebook ads. The results in the middle of the page are organic search results. These are important but we will save that for a different time.

When someone gets the result for searching "Albany Pool Supplies" they have the option of clicking on the links that most appeal to them. There is no guarantee that your ad will get clicked, you have to have a great headline, and body content that intrigues the prospect.

The 7 Steps to Set Up a Winning AdWords Campaign

#1 - Set Your Goals

You will want to determine exactly what you're looking to achieve with your campaign. Do you want a specific number of leads per month? Are you looking to increase inbound phone calls, newsletter signups, or make sales on your web site?

#2 - Do Your Research

Research the Keywords – Use keyword tools like Market Samurai or Google's Keyword Planner to find the most relevant keywords people are typing into the search engines to find your product/service/company.

Research Your Competition – You will want to spend some

time looking at the competition to see who consistently is ranking at or near the top of the rankings (you can use a spy tool like Keyword Spy Tool to help). Pay attention to their ad copy and offers. Visit their websites. Sign up for their mailing lists. Purchase their products.

Research Your Audience – Where are customers buying and reviewing products/services/businesses like yours online? Take a look at the reviews they are posting. What do they love/hate about your competition? What are the needs or desires they're looking to fulfill? While doing this part of the research you should be on the lookout for great quotes you can use for ad copy.

#3 The Landing Page Offer

An irresistible offer on your landing page it the absolute keystone to your AdWords campaign. While you were doing your research you saw what all your top competitors are offering. Now all you have to do is make your offer just a little bit unique/different/better. It is amazing what just a small improvement over the competition here can make!

#4 Use Exact Match Keywords

When first starting out with AdWords, you will want your keyword list very small (5 – 10 keywords) and very focused (the ones that people who are ready to buy are most likely to be typing into Google). Add all these keywords to your campaign as Exact Match keywords (this means that your ads will only be shown when someone types that exact term into Google). This way your ads will only show up for the most relevant searches and not for variations that Google may think are relevant, but aren't.

Over time, you can eliminate the keywords that aren't getting clicks/conversions and expand on the ones that are.

For example, if "Denver Dentist" is working for you, add more Exact Match variations of it to the list. Do this by combining the word "dentist" with zip codes, nearby cities, and by using variations like "dentists near Denver, CO", "best dentist in Denver", etc.

#5 Use Unique and Proven Ads

The ad copy should be highly relevant to the keywords they

show up for (including the exact terms when possible). Make sure you stand out from the competition by using different offers, benefits, etc. Your landing page offer should also reflect the same messaging as your ads to help people feel they are in the right place. If your landing page is not consistent with your ad copy it will hurt your conversions.

Test your ads. To do this you will place at least 2 ads in each ad group and then split test them. As a general rule of thumb, after each ad has at least 30 clicks, delete the lower performing ad and replace it with a new one.

#6 Track Your Results

Whatever the goals for your campaign, track your results.

Track downloads, newsletter signups, sales, etc. with AdWords conversion tracking. If phone calls are what you're after, use a Call Tracking service.

#7 Mine the Data

You get data from AdWords you can't get anywhere else. Take advantage of it.

You can use the keyword data to find keywords that are good

candidates for Search Engine Optimization (SEO) for your website.

As mentioned above, test different messages, headlines and offers in your ads. When you find ones that people really respond to, test them on your landing pages and in other marketing media.

Used this way the information you get from AdWords and Facebook Ads can be the grease that lubes your entire marketing engine.

As we will look at next, Google, Yahoo, and Bing each have their own internal list of local businesses, kind of like their own Yellow Pages. When you search on one of these search engines for a local business, part of the search is in their own list. To secure proper placement on these lists (and on the search engines' maps) you must claim and verify your business with each search engine and build out your listing to their specifications according to your type of business.

Strategy #3: Google+ Listing and Local Online Directories/Citations: Positioning Your Business Online

Local directories are web properties that allow businesses to list the details of their business at no cost. These directories can be vitally important for any local businesses. These listings can show up in the online search results and on apps on mobile phones like CitySearch, Google Maps, Yelp, and many more.

The reason this is critical for any local business is that according to a comScore-Localeze survey, 50% of Local Searches on mobile devices are done using these Directory Apps. It's like every person with a smart phone is walking around with access to 15 different phone books at their disposal at any second, right in the palm of their hand!

So which one is it most important to be listed in?

The simple answer is all of them!

You may have heard of Google+ because it is the largest local directory on the Internet. It actually gives information for local business as a listing in Google. This allows clients a way to actually show up on the first page of Google whenever someone searches for their industry and city. If you put in "Denver Dentist," as I mentioned earlier, it will show up with dentists in Denver that are on a map shown on Google.

Simply put: Google+ is the way for any local business to put information online and have it show up on the first page. As a matter of fact, there are businesses who don't even have a website who have first page Google listings because they have put the correct information on their Google+ page.

Many business owners are not as familiar with Google+ as they are with other social media websites. However, with approximately 343 million active users, the site is gaining in popularity and should be considered as part of your marketing plan.

One of the most popular aspects of Google+ is that it allows users to create circles. These circles can include friends, businesses, work colleagues, and customers. By creating different circles for each of these groups, you can then share specific information with a specific circle.

This technique allows you to create customer and business related content that you can then share in the respective circle. This is a great way for businesses to tailor their marketing plan to reach their target market using Google+.

Another benefit that Google+ has to offer is that it allows you to share coupons, announce new products, host contests, share blog posts, and publicize current promotions. This is a great way for businesses to share information that is relevant to their existing clients and helpful in attracting new ones. Businesses also have the opportunity to use their Google+ page as a way to humanize their business. This can be done by sharing videos or stories about your employees and what they do each day.

In addition to the benefits we have already mentioned, another important benefit to using Google+ is that it can have a positive effect on your online visibility. When people interact with your Google+ page or +1 your content, it is demonstrating to Google that people are interested in your business. When Google notices this, they will begin to reward your activity on Google+ with a higher search engine ranking. This means that when people search for a product or service that you offer, you will become easier to find and be placed closer to the top of the search results provided.

Another way that being an active member on Google+ can help your business is that when your posts are properly optimized, Google will take notice. To ensure that your posts are properly optimized, you should include keywords and topics that relate to your specific business niche. When optimizing your content, it is important that you include these terms in your content naturally. If you include too many keywords, or they do not flow organically they may have the opposite effect. Keep your content natural and organic and you will get the attention of Google.

Google+ is a valuable marketing tool for any business. If you are already using social media as part of your marketing plan you should definitely consider what Google+ has to offer. It is a great way to increase awareness about your business and attract new clients.

How to Get Google+ Reviews for Your Business

A Google+ listing for your business is an integral part of your internet reputation. It will be an invaluable tool for your online marketing plan. One essential factor is reviews.

Customer reviews can make or break you; they are what often provide others with the information to make a decision. You want plenty of positive reviews in order to make the most out of your Google+ listing.

The reviews you receive should be relevant, high quality customer accounts. So how do you handle this aspect of your Google+ listing? Below are some tips that will get you started; these tips will show you how to get reviews as well as respond to them.

Ask for positive reviews. This is simple. If you have satisfied customers, encourage them to visit your Google+ listing and write a review. Explain how easy it is to do and won't take very long. They will only need to click on the "write a review" button located at the top left corner of your listing and begin typing.

Google+ provides you with a link that is personalized just for your business. You can send it to your email and/or regular postal mail lists for the purpose of directing people to your listing. When doing this, be sure to ask for reviews. You should also include this link on all business correspondence as well as ads and marketing materials. This is another great way to promote your link and request reviews.

Generate a QR code linked to your listing. Place it on everything business related your customers may be likely to see. Include a simple request for them to post a review after visiting your listing. QR codes will take anyone accessing the internet via a smart phone directly to your Google+ listing with a quick scan. This process is easy and effective.

List your business in directories such as: Bing, Yelp, Foursquare and Yahoo. Business listings, and all other reviews that are submitted to those sites will be automatically linked to and will show up on your Google+ listing.

Responding to reviews is just as important as receiving them. Feedback is very important and can go both ways. Below are more useful tips. Unfortunately, there will always be people who are unhappy with your business no matter what you do. Sometimes these people will be unhappy with any business. Still, you will want to respond in a way that will preserve your reputation. Responding is the way to do this.

Respond promptly. This will show the negative reviewers you are paying attention to what they had to say. Make an attempt through your response to resolve any existing issues. Express your perspective in a way that isn't insulting or self-justifying.

You will, of course, get plenty of positive reviews. Always be sure to thank your satisfied customers for their support. In the case of your business, tell your patients how much you appreciate their great reviews. You might also offer public referral rewards and coupons to customers through the Google + listing forum. This will encourage potential customers to pay you a visit.

There are dozens of local (niche) directories available to any Local Business and in order for a listing to show up in the search results it must be consistently optimized similar to Google+ above. Each directory listing needs to have pictures and videos. The description of the business needs to be written exactly the right way. The features of the business and the categories all need to be listed in such a way that it gets the attention of local searchers. This allows you to show your hours of operation and directions to your location. People can push one button to call the store or get turn-by-turn directions from where they are straight to you front door.

Another powerful part of Local Directories are citations created by people leaving reviews of their experience with your business. Obviously, the higher the ratings and reviews, the more people like it, right? Think about the last thing you bought on Amazon, I'll bet you looked at the ratings other people had given the book or product. The same thing goes for your local business!

Strategy #4: Social Media - Facebook, Twitter, YouTube and More

The next traffic path is social media. There are a ton of these sites on the Internet and everyone looks at Facebook and Twitter as the two biggest players online. And for good reason, Facebook has over 1 Billion users and Twitter has over 300 Million active tweeters.

These platforms provide channels for getting information in front of tons of people. You can identify them and target them locally based on the geographic information; on both of those systems, people tell you what they do, what they like and where they live (most of the time).

Facebook is more social. You can advertise and put a wider variety of information there. Twitter is about marketing to the masses and small little bursts called tweets. With Twitter, you can only post a message that's 140 characters in length. With 140 characters, you don't have a lot of room to go into a detailed description. You can target your audience with tools like twellow.com to identify people who are in the city that you're dealing with.

Facebook provides a lot more demographic information on its users, which allows you to target your audience based on location, age, gender, relationship status, education, profession, and interests. Armed with this information you can develop ad campaigns and have them presented only to your ideal client.

For instance, if you were doing a golf ad, you would definitely want to cut the demographics down to where you want it. Let's say, you wanted to target female golfers in Baltimore, MD. You would probably select, obviously, females. You would select a range of probably 25 to 55. You might select college educated. And you would probably select married. This should all be based on solid research on your markets demographics.

Another aspect of social media is YouTube, and I'll talk about that a little bit more when I get into the video section, but YouTube actually is a social media platform because you can have subscribers, send messages, and leave comments. So it really does become a social media platform.

LinkedIn is a social networking site designed specifically for the business community. The goal of the site is to allow registered members to establish and document networks of people they know and trust professionally. The owner of the business needs to have a LinkedIn profile, and the business needs to have a company profile. There are some social aspects to LinkedIn, but it really is about business. It's about people who are in business, business owners, salespeople, and business professionals.

The main goal of all these sites is to direct people to your website, so make sure you're always leading them there.

On most social sites you can optimize profiles for local business. With Facebook you can set up a Facebook fan page, create a customized time line and create content for people to interact with. For a restaurant you could post pictures of the menu items; if it's a doctor's office, you might display before and after pictures of services. You always want your posts to leave customers saying, "Wow, this is business that I feel like I know, like and trust." You want them to be a fan of the page and ultimately become a customer of the business, product or service."

You can customize the background on Twitter, customize the feed, and customize the information you provide to your followers. The information that the business owner provides should be useful to the person who's viewing it whether they choose to do business with them or not. I'll reiterate this point a few times because it really is the key factor when it comes to creating a credible presence online.

The Power of Videos

Video is one of the most powerful means of putting information online. Why? Well, ask yourself this. What do people do more often, read books or watch television? Obviously, it's watch television because most people don't want to read. They're lazy and they like to be entertained.

If you look at YouTube, what are the videos that have the most views? They're entertaining, or they're providing information. They entertain; they're funny or controversial. Now, the other videos that get a lot of views are videos that provide great information in a way that gets people's attention. For instance, if you do a search on Google or

YouTube to figure out what causes the popping sound when you crack your neck, back or knuckles, you will find a chiropractor answering the question, "What's that popping sound?" It has over 120,000 views.

That's because people want to know what that popping sound is when the chiropractor adjusts them. Whenever you answer questions that people want know, it increases the video ranking. When you post a video you want to be sure to title it with the information of how people will search for it.

For instance, going back to our "dentist in Denver" example, you would want to put "Denver Dentist Explains Why Root Canals Hurt." That way you have the geographic identifier, you have the dentist part, and then you have what the description of the content. You also want to put in keywords and tags so that it gets people's attention and can possibly show up in the search engines.

The real value of video is having people find it in local searches, and it also provides you with tons of content that you can use to post on social media platforms.

What we've discovered is there's a lot of different ways to make videos. You can use animoto.com where you simply put pictures in, and it'll actually add music and create a video for you. You can make videos by using PowerPoint or Keynote, which is like PowerPoint for Mac. The simplest and easiest way to make a video is to use a digital camera or computer camera and record yourself answering questions that they get asked all time. These are called frequently asked questions. When you post these FAQ videos you will see favorable results, because people are usually looking for answers to these questions online.

Videos are very search engine friendly and can rank on the first page rather quickly with the right titling and tagging. Of course YouTube is the biggest video sharing site and the second largest search engine on the planet so it is very important to have your videos uploaded there, but YouTube is not the only player in town. It's also very beneficial to put videos on other video sharing sites like Vimeo, Viddler, Kewego, and more. There's a ton of them out there. You can simply do a Google search for video sharing sites, and you'll get an entire list of all the places that you can post videos.

Using YouTube to Market Your Business

Getting Started – To get started using YouTube, you will first need to create your channel. This step may require a little time, but the effort you put into creating and customizing the channel to suit your business will be well worth it. When you customize your channel, you should include your logo and customize the colors to those related to your logo and business. This will give your channel a customized look and help it be recognized by those familiar with your brand. During the initial setup phase, you should include the option of allowing users to subscribe to your channel. This will ensure that your target market is receiving your latest videos.

Types of Videos – Now that you've created your channel, you're probably wondering what types of videos to begin posting. The best types of videos for businesses tend to be how-to videos and FAQ videos. These types of videos will allow you to show your subscribers how to use your products in the most effective manner. You can also show uses for your products that your customers may not be aware of. How-to and FAQ videos are also a great way to drive traffic to your website.

Sharing – When you create your YouTube channel, you will then be able to share your videos across your other social media pages. Posting your videos on your Facebook page is a great way to show your customers that you are on YouTube and that your videos have something to offer. You can also share links to your videos in your tweets, which will help expand your subscribers to your YouTube channel.

Feedback – Each time that you post a new video, you can gain valuable feedback. Your customers will be able to leave comments about your video, products, or tips that you included in your video. This is a great way for you to see what is working and what you may need to change.

Online Visibility – YouTube is also a great way for businesses to increase their online visibility. When someone searches for a product or service that you offer or have mentioned in a video, your link will be presented in those search results. To truly benefit from this, you should be sure to include relevant keywords in your video titles. This will help increase the visibility of your videos and gain valuable exposure for your business.

YouTube Stats

- 4 Billion Views a Day
- Each Second 1 Hour of Video is Uploaded
- Each Month there are 800 Million Users
- YouTube has had over 1 Trillion Views
- YouTube Mobile has 600 Million Views Each Day
- Google bought YouTube in 2006 for $1.65 Billion

Strategy #5: Mobile Marketing – One of the Newest and Fastest Forms of Mass Marketing

Why is mobile marketing becoming so important? Well, let me ask you a question. Do you have a mobile device within arm's reach that you can access the Internet with? Go ahead. Think about it. I'll wait... Of course you do. Right now, within three feet of you, you probably have your cellphone. And that cellphone probably is a Smartphone... And that Smartphone has the ability to get online. You have a way of searching the web from nearly any mobile device.

When someone does a local search on a mobile device they usually make a purchase based on the information they find within 24 hours vs. a week or longer from a search on a computer. For restaurants it is usually within 60 minutes...
That is what we call a purchase driven consumer!

With mobile marketing there are a couple of ways to market information. The first is by creating a mobile website. If you look at a regular website on your iPhone or android, a lot of times they're jumbled up. They may look like it does online, but the screen is really small and you have to pinch and squeeze and move stuff around. And it's hard to navigate.

A mobile site really takes your website, cuts it down to about four or five pages of the most relevant information. That way, when someone goes to that website, they're able to navigate it very quickly. For instance, if it's a restaurant, it would have a contact us button, a menu button, a directions button, and maybe a specials button so that they can get to just the information that they're looking for. For example, for a restaurant website should have a takeout menu, because most people, when they go on their phone looking for food, it's takeout.

Another way to utilize mobile marketing is with SMS or text messages. With text marketing, you have to first capture the subscriber's phone number, and then you can then market to them over time utilizing text messaging.

Why is mobile advertising so important? Well here's the thing: only about 36% of emails get opened compared to more than 92% of text messages or mobile messages get looked at within the first minutes of being received. As a matter of fact, you've probably looked at your phone while you've been reading this report. That's the power of mobile marketing.

Using a Mobile App to Showcase Your Business

Yep... There's an app for that...

And today many local businesses are taking advantage of having an app made just for their business. A mobile app is a software application developed specifically for use on a wireless device like a smartphone or tablet rather than a desktop or laptop computer. The applications are housed on and made available on Apple and Google Play.

A mobile app for your business gives your customers the opportunity to have your business information loaded directly on their smartphones so they can interact with your business and receive specific communications.

Having a customized app allows businesses to:

Build customer loyalty - Make your customers feel special by offering discounts, coupons, and promotions just for using your app.

Send push notifications - Deliver instant messages to your customers' mobile phones whenever you wish. While only 4% to 10% of emails get opened, push notifications get read 97% of the time.

Create viral buzz - Let customers quickly tell all of their friends about you using the built-in sharing capabilities of Facebook, Twitter, LinkedIn, your blog, SMS, and Email.

Grow your list - Gather names and email addresses directly inside your app and easily export them into your favorite email marketing campaign service.

Promote special events - Provide up-to-date information about all of your business events, sales, and promotions with an in-app events calendar that anyone can access.

Gain more credibility - These are still the early years of the mobile app. Having one adds serious credibility to your business—especially among those who don't know how easy we make it.

Keep customers informed - Fill your app with information about your business, service offerings, product samples, menus, and more. There's a tab for just about everything you want them to know.

Connect with ease - Make it simple for customers to reach you using one touch calling, email, a website link, and GPS directions to your business—all from inside your app

Get instant feedback - Allow customers to leave feedback on your fan wall, share photos, make restaurant reservations, and send comments in a variety of ways.

Track your success - Use robust analytics to track daily, weekly, and monthly downloads of your app.

Another way to utilize mobile marketing is with SMS or text messages. With text marketing, you have to first capture the subscriber's phone number, and then you can then market to them over time utilizing text messaging.

MOBILE STATS

- Over 60% of Consumers use their smart phones to find local businesses.
- Mobile Phones will be used more than PC's
- Over half of consumers use their phones in stores for buying decisions.
- In 1-year smartphones users will be over 1.5 billion worldwide.
- Mobile search is predicted to be bigger than the Internet search next year.
- Over 70%+ of online retailers are developing a mobile strategy.
- Smart phone market is now bigger than the PC market.

XURLI.com/marketinganalysis

Strategy #6: Blogging - The Overlooked Local Marketing Tool

When most people think about blogging they think of a site focused on topics with a national scope. Locally focused blogs are powerful marketing tools for smart business owners. The power of the blog comes from the focus on the local community, which provides ample opportunities to use the city or town in the blog post headlines.

Blogs are very easy to create using one of the popular sites like Word Press or Blogger and with proper keyword placement the blog posts can easily rank on the first page of the search engines. Make sure your content has value to the audience you are trying to attract and be careful not to overload the posts with too many keywords. One example shows a blog post ranking #1 for "Poor Cell Reception Florida" out of 6.6 Million results... and they say blogging isn't effective.

Always post a variety of content that your audience will find interesting. If you only post information about your business and products & services you will lose the interest of most readers. Look for other local bloggers and offer them guest-posting opportunities on your blog. If Jimmy Fallon were the only person on the Tonight Show it would eventually get boring... Jimmy is an entertaining guy but the guests on his show are what add the variety that keeps it interesting.

Use pictures on your blog. People are very visual in nature and a blog post with pictures gets more interaction and than text only posts. You can also name the picture files with the keyword to increase optimization for the post.

Always ask for feedback. Engagement is very important with local audiences. Challenge your audience with questions and ask them to leave their answers and comments. This engagement will not only make things more interesting for the readers, it will also make the post more relevant to the search engines and you will be rewarded with better search rankings.

**Direct Response Marketing - How to Get More Business
Without Having to Get More Customers...**

The fortune is in... The Fishbowl?

Not the thing you were expecting right? Think about it... you go into a restaurant and they have a fishbowl on the counter at the register for you to drop in a business card to enter to win a free appetizer, lunch, dessert, or maybe ever free drinks.

What do you think happens to those cards after the remove them from the fishbowl?

NOTHING!

I can tell you from experience.

At this point you may be thinking that's great but we don't have fishbowls on our front counter. And you are right... But... EVERY business has a fishbowl, they just don't sit at the register and they don't look like fishbowls.

Remember the last time you went to the dentist or doctor and saw those patient folders along the wall behind the receptionist with the colored tabs on them?

Fishbowl!

Ever go into a business that had rows of customer files in 4-drawer file cabinets along a wall?

Fishbowl!

Oil Change companies put that little sticker on your windshield...

Fishbowl!

Excel spreadsheets with customer invoices and contact info...

Fishbowl!

EVERY business that collects contact information from their customers has a Fishbowl! Those customers willingly gave you their information and it is your job... your responsibility to tell them when you have an offer that they might find interesting.

Staying in touch with your customers is easier than you think!

There are very simple and inexpensive services called auto-responders that you can use to set up your client lists and send out communications to your customer base with the touch of a button. These systems can send email, text messages and some can even send recorded phone messages.

Strategy # 7: Email Marketing - Why an Automated Email System is Essential

These days, there are greater time constrictions on businesses which act to limit consistent marketing. Many of the limitations are due, in part, to fewer staff and tighter budgets. One of the greatest strategies to oppose this challenge is with the use of automated email systems for your vein clinic. These routine reminders are great for increasing website traffic and general sales.

Local businesses have seen tremendous results from this line of promotion and have abandoned antiquated and far more time consumptive methods of keeping in touch with clients. Understanding that workforce cutbacks and reduced line item funds for constant contacts are far more the norm than the exception, many companies have even eliminated them altogether. If you find your company with staff that plays dual roles, you understand the importance of managing time and labor.

The controlled management of your sales process is crucial. An effective way of administrating this process is through maintenance with preset systems that contact your entire population. Many of these systems have tracking and progress reporting as a regular function. You can either go with an experienced company, or hire an IT professional to build an individualized program that best meets your center's needs.

There is a popular saying that declares, "...if you build it-they will come." It might be wise to add that if it is built and never used or disseminated, they will turn and go in another direction. Do not shoot your business success in the foot by making the mistake of inadequately using the system in which you invested. Make certain that the email addresses of all your clients are current. Have it be part of the process when they enter your business for scheduled visits. Check regularly to see which messages are returned and eliminate those addresses. It is encouraged to send out several reminders or informative messages. Your clients may not participate or purchase from the first contact, but they may just be ready when the next one arrives.

Build the opportunity for client suggestions and feedback into the message. Tag a staff member to be responsible for responding to the comments. These responses should be done in a timely manner. It could mean the difference between a happy customer and a lost one.

After you have had some time to track and monitor the impact of your businesses automated promotions system, don't just sit on the information. Take the time to let it guide and instruct your marketing future. Did it meet your contact needs? Did you see an increase to your website visits? Did you see an increase in visits to your physical location or the sale of a particular product? These strategies are not only save time and cost; they work to inform your marketing practices and processes. You will only enhance the good work and for which your center is known. You will also give your clients the consistent and careful service and information they deserve.

Some of my clients tell me that their customers are different... They say, "my customers don't want to hear from me after they buy my product." Until they hear the following story...

An Unexpected Lesson in Follow-Up

In most places the government regulates power company operations. What that means is that if you don't have a choice who you buy electricity from, you have to buy it from the company that has facilities in your area. They are referred to as "regulated monopolies".

This means that no matter how upset you get with the power company, you have to either buy electricity from them or not have any... Let's face it, there are usually only two instances where you even think about the power company, when you get your bill each month and when the lights go out. Neither one is what you would call a positive experience.

In 2003 there was one such company whose customer satisfaction scores were not horrible but they certainly were not great. Then disaster when they got slammed with two of the worst hurricane seasons on record. They had back-to-back-to-back hurricanes that left the majority of their customers without power for weeks.

Then, because they had exhausted their $1 Billion Dollar Storm Re-Building fund (power companies can't get insurance on their power lines) they had to go to their customers and tell them that we would have to charge them 10-15% more each month to replenish the fund.

To add insult to injury, the cost of fuel went through the roof during this same time frame and they had to increase their bills another 30% within a few short months.

Needless to say they had to deliver bad news to these customers over and over again during an 18-month stretch from August of 2004 to February of 2006. They were dreading the day that the customer satisfaction ratings would come out for the company.

The Shocking Truth

When they received their customer satisfaction scores they were blown away, <u>the scores had improved to an all-time high!</u>

It turns out that because they were communicating so regularly with their customers, that even though they were calling/emailing/faxing to give their customers bad news, the customer's perception of the quality of service actually went up!

As a result they developed a 12-point communication plan so that now they are touching base with each major account at least once a month. In the next year they actually won an award for being best in class for customer satisfaction. So much for "no news is good news"!

What does this have to do with your company? Everything!

If customers who don't have a choice who they buy a service from get a sense of high customer support from increased communications... How much more impactful do think it can be for your business! From my experiences it is substantial!

Just imagine how happy your customers will be when they receive a message from you that you are having a sale, offering a new service, a VIP program, prize give-a-ways, or just sharing a helpful tip on how to get more value out of your product or service. If it works for a big old stogy power company it will work for you!

XURLI.com/marketinganalysis

Bonus Strategy: Reputation Management – What Are They Saying About Your Online?

Many business owners fail to recognize how important their online reputation is. It can make the difference between increased sales and a dramatic drop in sales. Just one negative comment or review is enough to dramatically affect your online reputation. Once your reputation takes a hit, you will likely see decrease in website traffic and the amount of sales you would normally experience. Below you will find some ways in which you can monitor and manage your online reputation.

In order to see what potential clients see when they search for your business, simply perform a search as they would. This will show you what is being presented to searchers and what is being said about you and your business. Regularly monitoring your online reputation will ensure that if there is any negative content being published you are aware of it. If you know what is being said about you online, you are in a better position to take control of the situation and manage how the content is being seen.

During your research, if you notice any negative post or comment that has been published regarding your business you should act quickly to minimize any negative effect it may have. One negative comment can be enough to cost you potential clients. No matter how hard we try as business owners, we have to realize that we cannot please everyone 100% of the time.

If you notice a negative post on any of your social media pages, you should address that comment immediately. The quicker you act to remedy the situation the less likely the unhappy customer will be to post any additional comments. If you choose to ignore the comment and not reply, the individual may continue to post additional comments, which can have a dramatically negative effect on your online reputation. The key is to act quickly and do everything within your power to solve the problem.

Taking a proactive approach to your online reputation can provide you with valuable insight into the type of content being published about your business and brand. The more involved you are in the process the easier it will be to notice any newly published negative content. Once you are aware of this content, the key is to act quickly and decisively. This will ensure that the negative content is taken care of and any further searches will present people with positive reviews and content.

There is nothing that can damage a business more than negative comments being posted online. However, if you are proactive and continue to monitor your online reputation, you will be better prepared to deal with these situations as they occur.

Google, Yahoo, and Bing are the places to start. Adding a SMARTsite and locking it to the listings gives you a fully compliant presence with the search engines. Now it's time to look outside the search engines and get more traffic and exposure. There are hundreds of alternate directories for every type of business that maintain listings as well.

Getting your business listed across all relevant directories accomplishes three things:

- Generates actual traffic and clicks from the individual directories, which often appear in search engine results
- Reinforces the accuracy of the information in the search engine listings themselves, which increases the amount of exposure the search engines give over time on specific local searches
- Broadens the geographic area in which most local businesses will be shown

Summed up differently, the search engines will look to the other directories to verify that the information they have on file (i.e., your listing) is accurate and supported by other sources. The more supporting sources they find, such as the directories or what we call "References" or "Citations," the more accurate, and consistent the information is, the more the search engines trust the information and therefore show the listing.

A Word on Branding

Properly branding your new business is one of the most important steps you can take on your way to successfully marketing your local business. Establishing your brand will inform potential clients of what your business does and who you are. One of the most important elements of your brand is your logo. It is what will become the face of your company and what people will associate with you and your business. Having consistency across all the platforms and strategies we have discussed is essential to portray a congruent brand.

When you properly brand your business, you will be able to set yourself apart from your competitors. Your business is unique, and it should be branded as such. This will also allow you to reach your target audience more effectively and create marketing plans centered on your brand. When properly implemented, a successful marketing plan will help you reach your target audience. This means those who can truly benefit from your particular products and services will hear your message.

Branding your business will also help you create an emotional connection with clients. When you emotionally connect with your clients, you will create a way in which they can identify and connect with your business. This can be achieved through the use of a well-designed logo and marketing plan. Your logo is what will identify your business; because of this the design should be something that is recognizable as your brand and identifies your business.

A well-established brand is also an effective way to create trust in your target market. If potential clients believe that you are a trustworthy business, they are more likely to purchase your products and services. A business that is properly branded will experience a greater response from their emails, advertisements, and newsletters. As more people become invested in your brand, they will be more confident in the products and services that you offer. This trust can then translate to an increased amount of website traffic and sales.

When you're creating your brand, you should focus on the long-term goals of your business. Your brand is not something that is only being created to serve a short-term goal. The brand that you build should be strong enough to last through expansions and time while remaining consistent. This is the long-term marketing technique that appeals to audiences now and in the future.

Your brand should be designed to enhance your business, while adding a sense of permanence and reliability to your business. Your brand is what will be used to identify you now and in the years to come; because of this, it should be something that will instill trust in the minds of your clients today and in the future.

Special Report Content: The 11 Essentials to Marketing Your Business Online

With the countless methods of promotion being enlisted in today's market, it is vital to make sure that your company stays in step. Marketing your business online takes planning, commitment and the decision to use the tools wisely. Here are 11 Essentials to keep in mind as you begin:

Essential 1

Before you begin your campaign, take time to carefully plan a strategy. What is your goal? What do you plan to gain? How much time can the company devote to research and analysis? One surefire plan is to start with the basics and grow from there.

Essential 2

Make certain that your SMARTsite and contact information on all web searches are kept current. Check all links and backlinks to make sure that they are validated and functioning. Remove any that aren't working to ensure that you get constant traffic, unhindered by bugs.

Essential 3

Treat your online plan and the maintenance as a legitimate department. Have 'department meetings' on a regular basis to appropriately monitor data and make needed adjustments. Assuming that automations and follow-ups will happen on their own will cause huge mistakes and could create missteps and missed opportunities.

Essential 4

Keep consistent in your contact. Make sure that the clients hear from you. Share the most pertinent information about your business and any important dates. Share your business success stories and new changes that may be on the horizon.

Essential 5

Make sure that your company's mission is always kept in the forefront. Test all content and other writings against it to ensure that they are aligned. Make sure that anyone you contract any of your marketing services to is also very aware of your mission. Have an approval process for content before it is allowed to be posted.

Essential 6

Use social media. Good news travels fast, but bad news travels faster. Make sure that the messages and social connection opportunities are a positive reflection of your business by finding clients who are willing to write positive reviews and comments on pages like Facebook and Google +.

Essential 7

Join a forum or create a blog that is geared specifically toward an audience for your business. Create a niche and use it often. The more visible your company is, the more traffic you get and the greater your connections and earning potential can be.

Essential 8

Make sure that your clients have a venue available that allows them to give feedback and suggestions. They will feel heard and become loyal to your company and your brand.

Essential 9

Program any of your client contact systems to key in on special dates like customer birthdays, the anniversary of them first visiting your company. The options for specialization are many. This, too, will build greater confidence in your business.

Essential 10

Make sure that your entire staff is involved and that they share their stories and mission with the same vigor and enthusiasm that you would; communication is key.

Essential 11

Don't let inactivity and outdated content destroy your hard work or your reputation. If it isn't relevant, delete it.

Now you have the principles and techniques to quickly grow your business. If you would like to expedite the marketing process explained in this book you can visit **www.Xurli.com** and we will help you transform your online marketing and establish you and your business as the expert in your area. You can also visit our site and register for an in depth marketing analysis.

To immediately begin to start

TRANSFORMING your Business with the

Strategic Online Marketing solutions

described in this book, contact us for a

complementary marketing analysis by

going directly to:

XURLI.com/marketinganalysis

www.ingramcontent.com/pod-product-compliance
Lightning Source LLC
Chambersburg PA
CBHW070836180526
45168CB00002B/850